CW00801886

1 MONTH OF
FREE
READING

at

www.ForgottenBooks.com

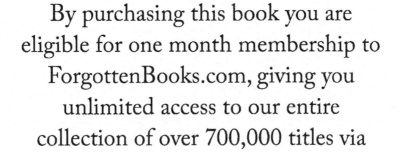

By purchasing this book you are eligible for one month membership to ForgottenBooks.com, giving you unlimited access to our entire collection of over 700,000 titles via our web site and mobile apps.

To claim your free month visit:
www.forgottenbooks.com/free129845

ISBN 978-0-260-43193-6
PIBN 10129845

BUST OF OLAVUS PETRI. MODELED BY JEAN LE VEAU.

OLAVUS PETRI

THE CHURCH REFORMER OF SWEDEN

BY

NILS FORSANDER

ROCK ISLAND, ILL.

AUGUSTANA BOOK CONCERN

ROCK ISLAND, ILL.
AUGUSTANA BOOK CONCERN, PRINTERS AND BINDERS.
1918.

To my Former Students in the Augustana Theological Seminary

BY God's grace alone are we justified and have eternal life, when in humble faith we behold Jesus, the Lamb of God, and follow Him. Thus we have cause also to cherish in grateful remembrance those of His servants who have preached His gospel in its purity to our fathers and to us. Hence it behooves us as a Lutheran people, for the better observance of their doctrines and precepts, to keep a steady eye on our great teacher Martin Luther at all times, and to give second place in our esteem to that foremost champion of Church Reformation in our Swedish fatherland—Olavus Petri.

In remembrance of our studies in Church History and Pastoral Theology, please accept, dear brethren, this guide to the life and teachings of the Swedish Reformer, Olavus Petri, "preacher of the Word of God." Brief as it is, it has been drawn from the best of historic sources. To Mr. Ernst W. Olson, for his services in rendering the manuscript into English, my grateful acknowledgment is due.

6

The work of Olavus Petri, this man of God, is more especially called to mind this year, the four hundredth from the time of his return to his beloved home land, from the halls of learning where Luther taught.

Yours, in the fellowship of Jesus Christ,

NILS FORSANDER.

Rock Island, Ill., Feb. 10, 1918, the four hundredth anniversary of the conferring the degree of Master of Arts upon Olavus Petri at Wittenberg.

CONTENTS

———

———

ILLUSTRATIONS

———

INTRODUCTION

THE Lutheran Church is dear to our hearts. We call ourselves Lutherans, not merely because of the fathers and teachers of this Church and the faith that was in them, but chiefly because Luther and his co-workers preached the pure and unfalsified gospel of Christ for the salvation of souls and administered the sacraments in the form and spirit implied by Him at the time of their institution, according to the same gospel. Christ is our Lord and Saviour, and in His name are we baptized; yet we are not ashamed to call ourselves Lutherans, inasmuch as that name stands for our belief in and confession of the doctrine preached by Luther unto repentance and faith in the forgiveness of sins through Christ. Luther and his co-laborers in the evangelical Reformation of the Church confessed themselves poor sinners saved by grace alone for Christ's sake and justified by faith in Him. Therefore these servants of God are very dear to us and esteemed worthy of being cherished in ever faithful remembrance.

Every Christian nation, like each individual believer, has received from God himself special gifts and a special calling, and the nation especially equipped leaders besides, for doing its part in the establishment and extension of God's kingdom. Thus He gave ATHANASIUS, that astute and subtle church father, to the wisdom-loving Greeks; to the Romans, those champions of law and an orderly government, He gave a stern and judicious ecclesiastical leader in the person of AUGUSTINE; and the peoples of northern Europe, protesting against tyranny and falsehood, and striving for freedom and truth, recognized in the bold but sensitive and conscientious MARTIN LUTHER their God-given leader and teacher and the Reformer of the Church. The Evangelical Lutheran Church of Sweden, which is not an annex to the Prussian Evangelical Union, but a sister church of genuine and faithful Lutheran churches, also has its racial characteristics as part of the true Church, namely, the heroic and earnest churchmanship already conspicuous in the first and foremost of Sweden's church reformers, OLAVUS PETRI. Him, therefore, we have every reason to recall to memory, to study, and to hold in high esteem.

We, the American Lutherans of Swedish stock, have received, by the grace of God and through the medium of the Church of Sweden, a most precious heritage from the Swedish church reformer, Olavus Petri. It was he who gave to our fathers, in the year 1526, the first translation into Swedish of the New Testament entire; in 1530, the first Swedish postil and catechism; in 1531, the first church book, essentially in the form still in use; and in 1536, that edition of his Swedish Psalm Book from which we have no less than twenty-two excellent hymns, still sung, in more or less revised form, in our homes and sanctuaries. How, then, could we forget our own Olavus Petri when we meet to celebrate our historic festivals to the glory of God and in memory of our great reformers?

Of this Swedish Reformer the learned Bishop J. A. EKLUND gives just appreciation in these words: "Olavus Petri is not only the greatest figure and the most richly endowed character in the renascence of the Swedish Church: his equal is not to be found in the Reformation history of the northern churches; he must be ranked next to the very greatest in the new era. That he has long been little known to the people of Sweden doubtless follows in a measure from our tendency to slight our own kin, but more especially from the fact that 'Master Olov' did not appear with pomp and loud acclaim. He was not, like BIRGITTA, a person of glowing zeal. He let the cause speak for itself. But if we listen closely, we will perceive a noble tone and lofty beauty in his simple, manly thoughts and words. The study of jurisprudence lent to his style the terse, austere ruggedness native to pristine Swedish speech." In a memorial entitled: "The Reformatory Fundamentals of Olavus Petri," published by Dean J. E. BERGGREN at the time of the erection of a monument to Olavus Petri at Stockholm, in 1898, the author styles him the foremost reformer of the Church of Sweden, and says of him: "The thought of what this man was able to accomplish in so short a time, and at a juncture rife with difficulties and untoward circumstances, cannot but compel our admiration." From other writers of the most recent period many quotations might be adduced to the same purport.

Not by violent appeal to men's feelings and passions, nor by rigorous laws and statutes, but alone by earnest preaching of the Word of God in its Scriptural purity and by zealous teaching of the gospel did Olavus Petri endeavor to impart to his countrymen the saving truth that makes men free in Christ Jesus. Besides this Swedish Lutheran evangelist in the true sense, we gratefully recall his two noted co-workers in the reformatory task, Archdeacon LAURENTIUS ANDREÆ of Strängnäs, subsequently chancellor to King Gustav Vasa, and LAURENTIUS PETRI, the younger brother of Olavus, known as translator of the Bible and as the first Lutheran archbishop of Sweden. Of MIKAEL LAGER-BEN, predecessor of Olavus Petri as rector of Storkyrkan in Stockholm, we know merely this, that he had been a student at the University of Wittenberg and was a staunch adherent of the evangelical doctrine. We are, however, bound to give King GUSTAV VASA a place here, for the support rendered by him to the reformatory work, especially during the early part of his reign. Praise and thanks be to the Lord for these men and for all leaders and shepherds of the Church of Christ!

I. STUDY AND PREPARATION

ACCORDING to memoranda made by himself or some chronicler of his time, Olavus Petri was born January 6, 1493, in Örebro, a city in the Swedish province of Nerike. It is further set down in the same memoranda that his parents were Petrus Olavi and Christina Laurentii. A statement giving 1497 as the year of his birth occurs as late as 1726, in J. G. HALLMAN, his first biographer, of whom Prof. HENRIK SCHÜCK, at present Sweden's foremost literary scholar, justly remarks that his sources are often found to be rather untrustworthy. We note the fact that the father of Olavus Petri was a blacksmith, as also that Martin Luther's father was a miner, and the father of Philip Melanchthon an armorer. So the life work of Luther was to bring the rich ore out of the deep shafts of Holy Writ. From the metal produced therefrom his co-worker Melanchthon hammered out the weapons used by the German theologians in their religious warfare and doctrinal controversies. To

Olavus Petri, the blacksmith's son, God assigned the work of shaping the same metal into plowshares wherewith to prepare the northern fields for the sowing of the gospel seed.

In his native town Olavus Petri received his schooling, either in the school connected with the Carmelite monastery, which was devoted to the training of monks, or in the city school, which dated its origin from the fourteenth century. His parents later sent him to Uppsala, where a university had been founded in 1477 by STEN STURE the Elder, regent of the realm, and Archbishop JACOB ULFSON. One of the most noted men of the university was Doctor PEDER GALLE, who subsequently became his shrewdest antagonist in the reformatory work. He himself had taught Olavus Petri the scholastic proofs and arguments on which the Roman Church based its alleged authority.

Owing to internal political strife and resulting lack of support from the state, the University of Uppsala was temporarily dissolved. In order to finish his studies Olavus Petri then went abroad and was enrolled in April, 1516, at the renowned University of Leipsic. Although he said little of his own spiritual experiences, we may infer that the soul of the young student was athirst for truth and peace. These treasures he did not discover in the sophistical lectures then given at Leipsic. Consequently he left after only a few months, going from there to Wittenberg, where a new university had been founded in the year 1502. We perceive in this the guidance of God, as we see the directing power of divine Providence in the invention of the art of printing, the revival of learning and the liberal arts, and the founding of a number of universities in the decades just prior to the Reformation of the Church through Luther.

Dressed in the cloak of an Augustinian friar, Luther in the spring of 1511 was on his way to Rome. At first sight of the city made sacred by the memory of martyrs, saints, and popes, he threw himself prostrate, then raised his hands with the words, "I greet thee, Holy Rome." While in the city, he eagerly sought out and visited all the places held sacred in the legends, and attended masses without number for the repose of souls. He is also said to have begun to climb on his knees up the twenty-eight steps of the Scala Sancta of the Sancta Sanctorum chapel, that traditional staircase of the court of Pontius Pilate by which Jesus is said to have been brought in for trial. Plenary indulgence was granted by the pope to all who performed that humble act of repentance. Halfway up the sacred staircase, Luther is said to have turned and descended, his conscience troubling him with doubts of the truth of the legends, and his mind revolting at the licentiousness of the priesthood and the monastic orders of Rome. While journeying back from the sacred city, Luther, by the grace of God, was gradually given to see clearly the truth of the Scriptural teaching, that a man is justified by faith.

In another way and for very different purposes, the young Swedish student traveled from Leipsic to Wittenberg at midsummer of the year 1516. He doubtless journeyed after the manner of other traveling students, so numerous at that time. These were distinguished by a feather in the hat, and they carried a long sword hung from a belt which was strapped tightly outside of a close-fitting coat. From one university to another they carried their books and other belongings in a wallet strapped to the back.

Wittenberg was a city neither great nor renowned, merely a little old town with narrow, crooked streets, and houses thatched with straw. The name is said to mean "white hill," and to have been derived from the hill of white sand on which the town was built. What attracted Olavus Petri to the place was the fact that Dr. Martin Luther taught theology at the university there. His reputation as the most skillful of interpreters of the Scriptures brought him this Swedish disciple, who came to satisfy his heart's yearning for righteousness and confirmation in divine truth.

The celebration in 1917 of the four hundredth anniversary of the Lutheran Reformation has recently called to mind the main facts of Luther's life and work; hence we may here confine ourselves to a brief account of his work in the three years, 1516—1518, during which Olavus Petri studied for Luther at Wittenberg. To the great advantage of himself and of his fellow countrymen, he now, through the grace of God, had the benefit of hearing his teacher clearly expound the Scriptures, and proclaim the gospel in spirit and in truth. They were not legends, fables, or papal decrees, these things that Luther presented to his students. He did not base his instruction upon human wisdom, but solely upon the firm foundation of the Word of God. "It is so written," that was Luther's watchword, and he submitted his faith and doctrine to the test of Scripture, not only at Worms, but also in the closet of prayer.

During the school year of 1516 Doctor Luther gave exegetical lectures on the Epistle to the Romans. The manuscript of these lectures was found in Rome as late as 1905 and was published at Leipsic in 1908. In Rom. 1:17 Luther had found his particular pearl of great price in the words, "The just shall live by faith." To him this implied the blessed assurance that God in His mercy and for the sake of Jesus Christ forgives us all our sins, imputes unto us the righteousness of Christ, and owns us as His children when with repentant hearts we believe in Him. Luther's convincing Scriptural theology and his lectures on the Epistle to the Romans worked a strong, constant faith and produced vital experiences in the heart of the newly arrived

GUSTAV VASA, KING OF SWEDEN.

Swedish student. Proof of this we find in the close inner correspondence between Luther's published exposition of the Epistle to the Romans and that published by Olavus Petri, entitled: "A Little Book in which is Explained how Man Gains Eternal Salvation, whether it be of his own Merit or purely by the Grace and Mercy of God" *(Een lijten boock ther vthi förclarat warder hwar igenom menniskian får then ewiga salighetena, om thet skeer aff hennes förtieniste eller aff gudz blotta nåde och barmhertigheet)*. This work is a clear and concise presentation of the author's evangelical Lutheran conception of faith, closing with an excellent summary of the Pauline doctrine compressed into fifty-seven brief evangelical theses or sentences. In the last three the relation between faith and works is set forth in these words:

"Wheresoever Holy Writ demands faith, there it means, not a vain, idle faith, but a faith which is active through love.

"Wheresoever Holy Writ demands good works, it means such works as proceed from a pure heart, not the works of an hypocrite.

"The whole life of man must be a constant offering of praise and thanks to God for His benefits, grace, and mercy. Praise and glory be unto Him forever. Amen."

Olavus Petri enjoyed the great and blessed privilege of often hearing Doctor Luther preach in the city

church. By request of the council of the city, Luther
served as assistant to the pastor of the parish from 1514
on. As such he sometimes preached four times of a
Sunday and two or three times during the week. In
the fall of 1516 he preached a series of sermons on the
Ten Commandments and another on the seven peniten-
tial Psalms of David. The latter series was published
in the spring of 1517, and this was Luther's first published work. In his preaching, Olavus Petri became
one of Luther's most faithful followers. He invariably
begins with a simple and lucid exegesis of the text, and
the central thing in his sermons is the evangelical testimony of Christ Jesus and the only and complete salvation of man through Him. In conclusion he gathers
passages of Scripture as a basis for an exhortation to
true faith, unfeigned love, loyalty to one's God-given
calling, and firm faith in the life eternal.

At the close of October, 1516, Luther began his
lectures on the Epistle to the Galatians, which were
continued during the year 1517, whereupon he lectured
on Hebrews and the Epistle to Titus the year following. In his exposition of the Epistle to the Galatians,
Luther arrived at a full comprehension of the right relation between the law and the gospel. This exposition,
revised and printed in 1519, is one of the most valuable
and instructive works in the literature of our Church.
Its powerful influence on the sermons and writings of

Olavus Petri is manifested, for instance, in the close of his brief but clearly Biblical explanation of the Second Article in his excellent catechism. There the author says:

"The sermon which deals with the Commandments requires much of us that we are unable to do. Neither does it lend power to fulfill that which is commanded. But the sermon which deals with faith carries with it grace and mercy. It tells us that God is willing to help us do that which the Commandments require of us, and even though all be not so fulfilled as it ought, yet He will forgive our shortcomings for the sake of His Son Jesus Christ, and of the indwelling of the Holy Spirit, regenerating and sanctifying us. Through the expounding of the Commandments we learn of the wrath of God; through the preaching on faith we are taught of His grace and mercy."

As professor of theology, Luther abandoned the then prevalent scholasticism, and all his students followed. When he was called upon to explain his position relative to the Roman traditions and legends, rules and decrees, and the papal claims to infallibility, he had no more faithful disciple and follower than Olavus Petri. He says in his work, "On God's Word and Man's Decrees" (*Om gudz ordh och menniskios bodh och stadhgar*): "God's Word is the Word of God as found in Holy Writ, which comprises all that man needs to know in order to be saved." The Scriptures are, according to him, the fountain of divine truth as well as of Christian life, "for of the Word of God is the life of the believer, and the Word of God is the food of the soul." Olavus Petri learnt also from Luther's teaching and directly from his example that the people must first be taught, before any reform of the superstitious abuses in church ceremonies and institutions should be undertaken. For we are told that in 1517 he had the valuable privilege of accompanying Luther upon his visitations to the Augustinian monasteries in Saxony and Thuringia.

It was in the midst of stirring and trying times that Olavus Petri pursued his studies at Wittenberg. In that city, poorly equipped as it was in a sanitary way, a plague broke out in the autumn of 1516, and during its ravages Luther was constantly occupied with the arduous and perilous task of administering aid and comfort to the plague-stricken.

Shortly after this infliction, JOHN TETZEL came to the vicinity and began the peddling of indulgences to replenish the exchequers of Pope LEO X. and Archbishop ALBRECHT of Mainz. The Elector of Saxony, however, would not tolerate this obnoxious traffic within the borders of his domain. The impudent and indecent pardon-monger plied his trade just beyond the Saxon border, selling indulgences for the dead as well as the living, and setting up the sacrilegious claim that his red cross, the sign of papal authority granted him, was as efficacious as the Cross on Golgotha, and that by his indulgences he had saved more souls than had both Paul and Peter with all their preaching. True, the Roman Church teaches that no indulgence can be conferred without confession and absolution, but Tetzel made provision for that by carrying with him a special father confessor who looked after that ceremonial detail in the same mercenary way.

Then came that memorable day in the history of the Christian Church, the thirty-first of October, 1517. In the afternoon of that day was held the celebration by which the people of Wittenberg commemorated the dedication of the Castle Church, the shrine of the diocese, on All Saints' Day. In that church, Elector FREDERICK, called the Wise, had collected a thousand alleged relics of sacred persons and objects, such as, a drop of milk from the breast of the Holy Virgin, a fragment of the staff of Aaron, a twig of the burning bush observed by Moses at Hebron, and the like. The teachers and students of the university, together with the people of the city and the surrounding country, were to be prepared by due ceremonies for viewing these sacred relics. Doctor Luther preached that afternoon on Luke 19:1ff, exhorting his hearers to give their hearts to God, that they might be dedicated as His temple.

When the multitude streamed out of the sanctuary there was in store for them a historic and more significant scene. On the door of the north entrance to the Castle Church was nailed a placard containing ninety-five theses on Indulgences, and these Luther offered to defend in public debate. The theses were written in Latin, according to the academic custom of the time, and when Luther had departed, doctors and students of the university gathered around. They read with astonishment his bold evangelical testimony to the only way in which God pardons sin — through repentant faith in Jesus Christ and His merit alone. The people throng about the students who one by one begin to translate and expound the theses to the ever growing multitude of listeners. In that moment Olavus Petri doubtless longed for an opportunity to expound these new truths to his countrymen at home.

From conscientious motives, not by any desire to set himself up as a reformer, did Luther compose and publish his theses. Among them were expressed truths which bluntly unmasked the fallacies of the traffickers in pardons, truths which burnt themselves into the minds and hearts of Olavus Petri and many other earnest seekers after divine light. The very first thesis read:

"Our Lord and Master Jesus Christ when He said, 'Repent ye,' willed that the whole life of believers should be a repentance."

The sixty-second was as follows: "The true treasure of the Church is the most holy gospel of the glory and the grace of God."

And the last two of the ninety-five were these: "Christians are to be exhorted that they be diligent in following Christ, their Head, through penalties, deaths, and hell;

"And thus be confident of entering into heaven rather through many tribulations, than through the assurance of peace."

The Ninety-five Theses of Luther comprised not only a stern sermon on repentance, but also an evangelical testimony to the grace of God through Christ toward poor sinners.

The theses were spread throughout Germany in a very short time. Within four weeks, copies reached nearly all parts of Europe. The Elector, who was peaceably disposed, made known to Luther his fears for the maintenance of peace. The prior and subprior of the Augustinian monastery in Wittenberg rushed to Luther in consternation, saying, "For the Lord's sake, do not desecrate our convent! The other orders, the Dominicans in particular, are already rejoicing over our shame." Luther answered them in these words, "Dear fathers, if this cause be not begun in the Lord's name, it will come to nought. If it be of the Lord, let it have its course." On the other hand, Prior FLECK of Steinlausitz, when he had read a number of the theses, exclaimed in delight, "Aha! he has come at last, the man for whom we have waited so long. He will do it."

In the city of Frankfort, Tetzel on January 21, 1518, posted his fifty counter-theses, one of which embodied his old stock argument, thus: "Whosoever denies that the soul flies out of purgatory so soon as the penny jingles in the money-box, that man is a heretic." He said further that Luther ought to be burnt at the stake, and himself arranged a mock auto-da-fé, in which he solemnly consigned Luther's theses to the flames. Tetzel was then made a doctor of theology, and copies of his fifty theses were circulated broadcast. Many reached Wittenberg, where the students gathered three hundred copies and, unbeknown to the faculty, burnt them in the public square amid great jubilation, but to Luther's sorrow, when he learnt of the prank.

Not one of the pope's creatures dared to engage in public discussion with Luther on his ninety-five theses. Archbishop Albrecht of Mainz and the Dominicans, however, lodged a charge of archheresy against him with the pope, and PRIERIAS, the Dominican father confessor of Leo X., justified the blasphemous sentences of Tetzel and added sundry pronouncements of equal authority, such as this: "Whosoever does not base his teaching on the doctrines of the Roman Church and the Pope in Rome, as the infallible rule of faith from which even the Scriptures derive their authority, is a heretic." And this: "We have knowledge of indulgences, not by the authority of Scripture, but by the authority of the Roman Church and of the Popes, which is greater." Luther's answer to all this was a forceful assertion of the supreme authority of the Canonical Books of the Bible in all matters pertaining to the Christian faith.

Through the machinations of Prierias and HOGSTRA-TEN, the inquisitor-general, Luther in June, 1518, received a summons from Rome to appear in person and answer for himself before "the supreme judge of the Church." To go would have been equivalent to mounting the pyre. The Elector of Saxony consequently secured the concession that Luther might stand trial before CAJETAN, the pope's representative, at Augsburg. This man had received in advance a papal bull putting Luther under the great ban and granting plenary indulgence to all who would aid in yielding him up to the papal authorities. Luther expected to meet the fate of HUSS, yet he went to Augsburg in the fall of 1518. There he retracted nothing, merely asking that his utterances and writings be submitted to the test of Scripture. Finally he secretly disappeared from Augsburg and subsequently appealed, first to the pope, "who ought to be better informed," then to a general council of the Church. Later, in the disputation with Doctor JOHN ECK in Leipsic, July 4—19, 1519, Luther placed the authority of the Holy Scriptures above that of church fathers, church councils, and of the pope himself. That was the true declaration of independence of evangelical Protestantism.

During these turbulent years, 1517 and 1518, Doctor Luther continued to preach and lecture as before. In a letter to Doctor J. LANGE, in July, 1517, he states that he was preparing six or seven candidates for the Master's degree. One of these, apparently, was Olavus Petri, who was promoted to the degree of A. M., at Wittenberg, February 10, 1518. By the manly and yet humbly Christian example of Luther during the years 1516—1518, Olavus Petri was being developed into a like champion of faith, equally fearless in combating the open tyranny and secret wiles of the devil and his henchmen. Our Swedish Reformer was taught the use of the whole armor of God, as described by Paul (Eph. 6: 13, 17), the breastplate of righteousness, the shield of faith, the helmet of salvation, and the sword of the Spirit, which is the Word of God. Thus equipped, Olavus Petri all his life remained a true champion of the truth, strong in the Lord and in the power of His might. He was withal a faithful and humble Biblical scholar, who gloried in nought, save in the cross of Christ.

Olavus Petri is known to have stayed in Wittenberg beyond the time when Luther returned, hale and nothing daunted, from Augsburg on the anniversary of the publishing of his theses, October 31, 1518. Thus Olavus Petri had an opportunity to study Greek for Master PHILIP MELANCHTHON, who came in August of that year and assumed his chair four days after his arrival, with a lecture which was highly prized by Luther. His studies for the learned Melanchthon were greatly to Olavus Petri's advantage when later, with the aid of the Latin translation by ERASMUS and Luther's German version of 1522, he translated the New Testament out of the original Greek and published it anonymously in 1526, under the title: "The New Testament in Swedish" *(Thet Nyia Testamentit på Swensko)*.

In November, 1518, Olavus Petri left Wittenberg, arriving in Strängnäs the following month. There he took a position as teacher in the cathedral school and was made chancellor to Bishop MATTIAS GREGERSON. By him he was ordained a deacon in September, 1520.

A hawker of indulgences, named JOHN ANGELUS ARCIMBOLD, had carried on the nefarious traffic among the Swedes in 1518, as had Tetzel among the Germans. This had been allowed to pass unchallenged, owing in part to the spiritual stupor and profound superstition of the people, and in greater part to the war with Denmark and the internal political conflicts which were absorbing the public interest. The regent, STEN STURE the Younger, was under the ban, together with all his supporters, for having deposed the traitorous Archbishop GUSTAV TROLLE, in 1517, by a vote of the states-general. Although burning with zeal for the spiritual welfare of his people, Olavus Petri was thus for some time prevented from carrying on any work for religious betterment. In the meantime he was attaining his spiritual maturity and learning the patient art of biding the Lord's time and His calling.

Olavus Petri accompanied Bishop Mattias to Stockholm to attend the coronation of the Danish king, CHRISTIAN II., as hereditary king of Sweden. Thus he became an eyewitness to the ghastly butchery of November 8—10, 1520, known in Swedish history as the Stockholm Blood-bath, a massacre executed by direction of the new union king subsequently known as Christian the Tyrant. At the instance of Gustav Trolle, who sought restitution and proffered the charges, a court headed by JENS BELDENACKE, a Danish bishop, was established to try the opponents of Trolle. The wily Danish prelate lost no time in convicting the defendants of heresy. Bishops Mattias of Strängnäs and VINCENS of Skara were the first to be beheaded; then followed the lords of the realm and eighty-two of the councilmen and chief citizens of the capital, and last their servants and friends, the bodies of all being finally burnt on a great pyre. When Olavus Petri was overheard expressing horror at this wholesale slaughter, he was immediately dragged into the enclosure surrounding the condemned victims, and he escaped, as by a special act of Providence, on the bare testimony of a German who knew him from Wittenberg and protested that he was a citizen of Germany.

· Olavus Petri, or, as he was now popularly called, Master Olov, returned to Strängnäs and in 1521 began publicly to preach the evangelical faith and to lecture to certain candidates for the ministry and younger pastors on portions of the New Testament. Among hearers won over to the cause of the Reformation were Archdeacon LAURENTIUS ANDREÆ, vicar of the diocese of Strängnäs, and LAURENTIUS PETRI, a younger brother of Olavus, who presumably studied at Wittenberg in 1527 and subsequently was consecrated as the first Lutheran archbishop of Sweden. Doctor NILS ÖSTGÖTE, dean of Strängnäs, who vainly opposed Olavus Petri, devised eight points from the teachings of Master Olov, which he construed as heresies, seeking to substantiate his charges by copious quotations from legends, church fathers, etc. In complete accord with Luther's principle for reading and interpreting Scripture, Olavus Petri is alleged to have made these assertions:

"In authentic writing there is nothing said of St. Anna as being the mother of the Virgin Mary.

"There should be no mendicant friars, that being contrary to God's order according to Deut. 15: 4.

"Put not your trust in any human being, such as the sainted Virgin or any other saint, but trust in God alone. Jer. 17: 5."

Doctor Nils sent his charges against Olavus Petri to Bishop HANS BRASK of Linköping. When this eminent divine learnt that Master Olov quoted Paul as an authority, he is said to have exclaimed, "Paul were better burnt than by all men learnt." These damning words the prelate took care not to repeat later in his official report.

While Olavus Petri was engaged in this preparatory work, Gustav Vasa had, as regent, with the aid of "God and the Swedish commonalty," liberated Sweden almost completely from Danish oppression. At Strängnäs, in the summer of 1523, he held council with the states-general, who on the sixth of June chose him king of Sweden. Then and there the newly elected king learnt for the first time of Luther and the Evangelical Reformation, this through sermons preached by men who had studied under Master Olov, and through Archdeacon Andreæ, who assured King Gustav I. that Holy Writ, to which Luther and Olavus Petri appealed, did not contain one word about the worldly power of the pope and the bishops, but taught, quite to the contrary, that these were to be the servants of the Church. To the opinion thus expressed by the archdeacon, on the relation of the Church to the secular power, Gustav acceded. Not long after, Andreæ was made secretary to the king and a member of the Council of the Realm. In the spring of the following year, Olavus Petri was appointed secretary of the city of Stockholm. As a member of the city government he advocated modern humane and evangelical methods of administering civil and ecclesiastical justice in place of the old system of torture. He maintained that all punishment should look to moral improvement, and held that it were better to acquit than to convict, in case of doubt, giving his reason thus: "It is far better to set a prisoner free than to inflict pain and torture on one who is innocent." It was no doubt under impressions received in the service of the city that he later wrote his "Rules for Judges," which have been reprinted as a preface to most editions of the "Law of the Swedish Realm." Among the rules this one is found: "A deed must be judged according to the intent of the doer, whether it was done with malice aforethought, or no." He reminds the magistrates that they are the Lord's overseers, who are not the judges of their own subordinates but of God's people.

Simultaneously with the royal election there arrived at Strängnäs the papal legate, JOHANNES MAGNUS, a native of Linköping, with a mandate to crush out the

Lutheran heresy in Sweden. Finding that he was able to do nothing, he was about to return to Rome to be invested with greater authority, when he was elected archbishop by the Uppsala chapter. Now it became a matter of prime concern for him to obtain the sanction of the pope for himself and four newly elected bishops. When he was on the point of starting for the sacred city, however, a mandatory brief from Pope HADRIAN arrived, ordering the reinstatement of Archbishop Trolle, or dire ecclesiastical punishment would follow. To this the king replied, on October 4, 1523, that if His Holiness insisted on forcing upon the Church in Sweden an archbishop who, in co-operation with King Christian, had perpetrated the atrocious murder of two of its bishops, he would "freely exercise his royal authority in so governing the churches and regulating religious matters in his realm as seemed most pleasing in the sight of God and acceptable to all Christian princes;" for he would not tolerate that his people "be made serfs under the heavy yoke of foreign oppressors."

Pope CLEMENT VII. consecrated PETRUS MAGNI as bishop of Västerås, upon his promise to pay the customary fees; but when onerous exactions were demanded from the other newly chosen bishops as the price of papal sanction, Gustav I. would not permit payment of the fees. Thereby the king, too, broke with the pope. Now Bishop Brask appeared against the reformers, re-

Swenske song=
ger eller wisor nw på
nytt prentade / fordz=
kade / och vnder
en annan skick
än tilförenna
vtsatte

Stocholm

MDXXXVj

TITLE PAGE OF PSALM BOOK OF 1536.

newing his order prohibiting the reading and circulation of the writings of Luther and the Reformers, at the risk of excommunication. He further requested that a royal edict be issued against lending aid and comfort to Luther's followers. King Gustav replied that Luther's writings had not been refuted or condemned by impartial judges, and that it was the duty of the king to protect all his subjects from violence and arbitrary interference with their rights.

Olavus Petri early in the year 1525 was joined in wedlock to a pious maiden, named Christina, five years older than himself. As a consecrated deacon he was pledged to celibacy for life, hence this was a brave reformatory step, in open defiance of the Roman Catholic law of celibacy, an enactment responsible for untold immorality and misery, and a curse to the Church. When this reached the ears of the king, he summoned Master Olov into his presence. The latter replied that he was prepared to answer before a court of impartial judges. When the information reached Brask, the irate bishop wrote a sharp letter to the king, demanding that so defiant an act be summarily punished, pointing out that Olavus Petri must be put under the ban in accordance with the law of the Church. This was King Gustav's trenchant answer to the bishop:

"To our limited understanding it seems peculiar that a man should be banned for the sake of marriage, which is not prohibited by the law of God, while members of the clergy are not put under the ban for illicit intercourse, according to the laws of the pope."

During his service as secretary to the city council of Stockholm, Olavus Petri preached regularly in the church now known as Storkyrkan, as vicar to Master Mikael Lagerben, the parish rector. He was popularly known as "Master Olov in the basket," owing to the basketlike appearance of his pulpit. There he was frequently greeted with the throwing of stones by the faithful Romanists, who thus proved their "righteousness by works." Of this Laurentius Petri subsequently wrote: "The preachers were obliged to stand the fire of the opposition and were made the targets for the poisoned arrows of many a murderous tongue; for at that time those were held to stand highest in favor with God who were loudest in vilification of the Lutherans as heretics, forfeiters of the faith, traitors to God, and such other infamies as they were able to devise." Master Olof, however, by his humble yet fearless appearance and by the spiritual power of his evangelical preaching, gained for himself the confidence of the saner element of the population.

In order to meet the needs of the government, the king placed several monasteries under the administration of the crown, whereupon a number of monks went as missionaries to Lapland and several monks and nuns entered matrimony. In 1526 the king assumed charge of the Gripsholm monastery as his hereditary estate. He sought to win over the nobles by promising to return to them such ancestral estates as their forebears had donated to the Church under false threats of purgatory drummed into their ears by priests and monks. The common people, however, were attached to their monks and priests, and the hard times prevailing throughout the country they charged to the king. Two prelates which had been deposed for disloyalty, namely, Bishop PEDER SUNNANVÄDER and Master KNUT, availed themselves of the overwrought state of the public mind for fomenting a revolt among the Dalecarlians. The king succeeded in quieting the province and capturing the two instigators of the uprising, who were convicted on evidence furnished by the crown, and executed in 1526.

Bishop Brask warned his clergy against infection from "the Lutheran, or rather the Luciferian, heresy," but the king forbade him to print and circulate any matter whatsoever without first submitting it for royal approval. Archbishop JOHANNES MAGNUS traveled about his diocese with a retinue of two hundred people. At a great feast, arranged by him in Uppsala at Whitsuntide, 1526, he is said to have proposed a health to the king in these proud words: "Our Grace drinks to Your Grace." The king left the hall in anger, with the explanation: "Our Grace and Your Grace cannot be housed under one roof." Going shortly afterwards on a royal mission to Poland, the archbishop never again returned to Sweden. The administration of the archbishopric, which he had turned over to Bishop Brask, was entrusted to Laurentius Andreæ.

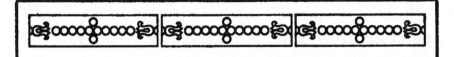

II. LITERARY ACHIEVEMENTS OF OLAVUS AND LAURENTIUS PETRI

PRIOR to the year 1526 less than ten publications in the Swedish language had left the press.

The very first, published in 1495, was a translation of John Gerson's work "On Temptation of the Devil;" the second, of the year 1514, was a translation of a little book by the same author, entitled, "How to Die unto the Salvation of the Soul."

The reformatory work of Olavus Petri began in a literary way in 1526, with the anonymous publication of three smaller works and his translation of the New Testament. "A Book of Useful Instruction" *(Een nyttwgh wnderwijsning)* was the title of his first reformatory work, published in February, 1526. It was based in part upon Luther's Prayer Book of 1522. The author closes with a promise that the readers would soon be given the New Testament in Swedish, adding an admonition to pray for the enlightenment and blessing of the Holy Spirit through the Word of God. "A Book of Beautiful and Useful Instruction" *(Een skön nyttwgh vnderwisningh)*, published the following year, was a short catechism, translated, presumably by Olavus Petri, from a Hussite original in Low German. This was later supplanted by a catechism worked out by Olavus Petri himself. The same year he published the first Swedish Psalm Book, containing ten psalms, four being from his own pen. This hymnody, augmented in the editions of 1530 and 1536, was instrumental in teaching the Swedish people how to worship God and propagate the evangelical truth in song.

The most important work by Olavus Petri published that year was, however, his translation of the New Testament. "Its appearance was undoubtedly the greatest single event in the history of Swedish literature." In his "History of Swedish Literature," Henrik Schück, Sweden's great scholar and literary critic, has this to say: "By his noble and considerate usage of the language the translator immediately raised our mother tongue and its orthography out of the disorder and clumsiness of Swedish orthography and syntax in the Middle Ages."

Through this translation the Word of God was made the actual possession of the people of Sweden, who now were enabled to read for themselves the eternal truths heretofore obscured by the superstition, the pitiful legends, and the gospel of good works taught by the Church of Rome.

With becoming modesty Olavus Petri did not put his name on this translation when it was issued from the Royal Printing Office. Yet the learned historian MESSENIUS (d. 1637) certified that it was the work of Olavus Petri, and so do all subsequent researchers and critics. The tradition crediting Laurentius Andreæ with the translation has been abandoned as groundless. A literal reproduction of the first edition was published with aid from the crown and from the Swedish Academy in 1893, in connection with the quadricentennial of the birth of Olavus Petri and the three hundredth anniversary of the Council of Uppsala.

The Swedish New Testament of Olavus Petri was published with a foreword comprising a translation of Luther's introduction to his German edition, with the elimination of the last part, containing his estimate of the different books, especially the Epistle of James, together with the Swedish translator's own reasons for rendering the Scriptures into the Swedish tongue and his explanations of certain words and fundamental gospel terms. In the foreword we read: "For this reason the New Testament is now issued in the Swedish tongue, the Old to follow soon, with the help of God, so that poor, humble preachers, who are little versed in Latin, and unacquainted with the Scriptures, and like-

wise other people who are able to read, may here be
given at least the plain text, such as it was written by
the Evangelists and Apostles... Perchance this version
may at a later day be amended and set forth more clearly and with less difficulty than has been done at this
time. In the meantime, this present version may well
be regarded fit for use; nevertheless it is not forbidden,
where anything herein may be found amiss, by over-
sight of the translator or printer, or not so well put as
it ought, for anyone with a right understanding to cor-
rect the same; this the present interpreter does not take
as a reflection upon himself, asking rather that it be
done."

The first work published by Olavus Petri under his
own name was his "Answer to an Unchristian Missive"
(*Swar vppå jtt ochristelighit sendebreff*), dated March,
1527. This is his most polemical work. The occasion
for it was given by a mendacious letter to the Danish
earl marshal TYGE KRABBE, written by PAUL HELIÆ,
a Danish Carmelite friar, who at first was well disposed
toward Luther but later turned traitor to the Reformation cause. This letter, widely circulated in Sweden,
made an attack on Luther so utterly unfair and malev-
olent that Olavus Petri felt in duty bound to defend
his beloved teacher. His defensory writing gives evidence of intimate acquaintance not only with the most
recent works of Luther but with the writings of his

antagonists as well. Heliæ sought to prove Luther responsible for the Peasants' Revolt in south Germany; Olavus Petri refutes the charge by presenting Luther's truly Biblical doctrine of Christian liberty. He goes on to show that the domineering spirit of the pope and the prelates was the underlying cause for civil strife and bloodshed, pointing out that Luther had reproved the rulers and princes for the tyranny exercised over the people.

A few months later there issued from the same office another book bearing the name *Olavus Petri,* the title of which was: "Answers to Twelve Questions on Certain Points in Which the Evangelical Teaching and the Doctrine of the Papists Do not Agree" *(Swar påå tolf spörsmål om noghor stycke ther then euangeliske lärdom och the papisters lärdom jcke dragha offuer eens).* In order to settle the unrest caused by evangelical preaching, Gustav I. caused to be formulated and circulated first ten, later twelve questions to be answered. A copy was sent in due course to Doctor Peder Galle, to be answered before Christmas Eve, 1526, which he did, as did also Olavus Petri. When the latter requested an oral disputation on the same points, Galle declined, although Olavus Petri went twice to Uppsala for that purpose. He was, however, given an opportunity to defend his teachings before the king and his council. Afterwards the written answers of both men were published, together with a refutation of Galle's tenets. The twelve questions were:

1. Whether one may ignore such teachings of holy men and such church usages as are not in agreement with the Word of God.

2. Whether our Lord Jesus Christ gave to priests, popes, bishops, and others, any power or authority over men but this, that they shall preach His Word and interpret His will; also, whether there should be any other priests than those who so preach.

3. Whether their laws, edicts and statutes, if broken, are able to retain unto any one his sins.

4. Whether they have the power by means of the ban to separate anyone from God, as a severed member of the Church of God, and to give him over to the devil.

5. Whether the present principality of the pope and his following be for or against Christ.

6. Whether there be any other way of serving God than to keep his commandments; as by observing man-made rites not ordained by God.

7. Whether man is saved on his own merit, or through God's grace and mercy alone.

8. Whether there be any foundation for monastic life in Holy Writ.

9. Whether any man now has or ever had the power to prescribe otherwise in regard to the sacrament of bread and wine than Christ himself ordained.

10. Whether one ought to put faith in alleged revelations other than those recorded in the Scriptures.

11. What support the Scriptures give to the doctrine of purgatory.

12. Whether one ought to worship and pray to the saints, and whether they are our defenders, patrons, mediators, and intercessors before God.

As against the power of the prelates, Olavus Petri asserts the common priesthood of all Christians, manifested in their right and duty to pray for one another and to comfort and reprove each other according to Scripture. Olavus Petri taught and maintained that the priesthood is a ministration of the Word of God, not worldly domination.

Paul Heliæ, after having received the Twelve Questions from the king and the answers by Peder Galle and Olavus Petri, wrote a letter to the king, warning him against the Lutheran doctrine and adding a sharp rebuke for his avarice. To this Olavus Petri in 1528 made answer in a pamphlet entitled, "A Brief Letter to Pàul Heliæ of the Carmelite Order in Denmark" (*Itt fögho sendebreff til Paulu Helie aff Carmeliters orden j danmarck*). Being quite bitter in tone throughout, it closes with this explanation: "That I have here and in my former writing on this subject spoken somewhat harshly is not, I admit, in accord with Christian meekness, but rather with your rancor...I have spared you, however, and assure you that hereafter I will not treat of these matters in this wise. The honor and vainglory derived from blasphemous and scornful words I do not covet." The subsequent rejoinder of Heliæ was left unanswered, and thenceforth Olavus Petri abandoned polemics. Far from being a hot-headed and violent apologist, he refrained more sedulously than any of the other Church Reformers from bitter words and harsh judgments of his adversaries.

The same year Olavus Petri published his Coronation Sermon, (*En Christelighen formaning till Sweriges jnbyggiare,* etc.), preached at the crowning of Gustav Vasa as King of Sweden at Uppsala in January, 1528. The text was fitly chosen from Deut. 17: 15—20: "Thou shalt surely set him king over thee, whom Jehovah thy God shall choose: one from among thy brethren shalt thou set king over thee; thou mayest not put a foreigner over thee, who is not thy brother," etc. He earnestly admonished the subjects to give obedience to their king, and cautioned the monarch, on the other hand, to bear in mind that "he is set as a ruler, not over his subjects, but over his own brethren, who are God's people."

Shortly afterward he published "A Christian Admonition to the Clergy" (*Een Christelighen formaning till clerekrijt*). With the words of Christ, "The good shepherd giveth his life for the sheep," as a motto, he sets forth "what the clergy owe to the laity, and what the laity owe to the clergy." In true Reformation style the author shows it to be the duty of the former to preach the Word of God, pure and simple, and of the latter to submit to those who teach them the Word and to see to it that they are properly provided for.

Although this work treated of the ecclesiastical conditions of the time when it was written, it contains many truths applicable even in our times, no less to the Roman Catholic hierarchy than to the still dominant spirit of avarice and worldly-mindedness. A few excerpts may therefore very properly be given as a part of Olavus Petri's testimony to unalterable truth.

"Thus says Paul (Acts 20: 28): 'Take heed unto yourselves, and to all the flock, in which the Holy Spirit hath made you bishops, to feed the church of the Lord which he purchased with his own blood.' Here he exhorts the ministers most earnestly to take heed unto themselves lest they accept some false doctrine and thereby lead their flocks astray. They must also take heed to the flock lest it be seduced and corrupted. This is the inexorable duty of the ministers, whom the Holy Spirit hath made bishops, or overseers, that is to say, custodians or superintendents, to guard His Church. This is indeed no mean office, for He hath appointed every minister of the gospel a bishop, and that not over some trifling thing, but over the communion of God himself, which He hath so highly prized as to have bought and redeemed it with His own blood. Over this communion are they made priests and bishops, terms in which the same office is implied. For a parish priest, placed as leader of God's communion, the Scriptures speak of as a bishop, that is, an overseer. From what has now been said it appears clearly what the priesthood is. It is an office, the holder of which is commanded by God and strictly ordained to preach the Word of God. This is the chief duty of his office; therefore, if he neglects to preach, he neglects his entire office.— — —

"Inasmuch as God hath so great zeal of His Word, that it be preached, the Scriptures praise those ministers who preach it faithfully. They are called good, wise, blessed, and faithful servants; they are said to be doubly worthy of honor; and the promise is given them that they shall receive eternal life, and an everlasting crown, and shall be placed over all the things that are God's; in short, they have promise of all that is good. As the faithful preachers are thus highly lauded, so those who preach unfaithfully or not at all are condemned and threatened with eternal perdition. The Scriptures call them lazy, faithless servants, wolves, knavish hirelings. It is therefore a fearful and perilous thing to make a pretense at the ministry and yet not preach as required by that office. Thus saith Paul: 'For if I preach the gospel, I have nothing to glory of; for necessity is laid upon me; for woe is unto me, if I preach not the gospel!' Now, just as it was a necessity laid upon Paul to preach, and he would have merited condemnation for not preaching, so also with all ministers, for they all have the mandate of God to administer His office. Woe unto them, if they preach not! That is a fearful and terrible judgment. — — —

"The Apostle Paul saith (1 Cor. 9: 13): 'Know ye not that they that minister about sacred things eat of the things of the temple, and they that wait upon the altar have their portion with the altar? Even so did the Lord ordain that they that proclaim the gospel should live of the gospel.' From these words one may well gather that those for whom the Word of God is being preached are in duty bound to provide the preachers with sustenance and a livelihood. They, therefore, who shirk their duty, withholding their due share, act contrary to the commandment and ordinance of God. For Paul plainly says in these words, that the Lord hath so ordained that even as under the old covenant they that served in the temple and officiated at the altar should live of the things of the temple and the altar, so also shall they that preach the gospel receive their support therefrom. He who shirks in this respect evades the ordinance of God and is unworthy of having the gospel preached to him. — — —

"The laity ought also to show that they cherish that which is preached to them, so that they act accordingly; and even though they may discover some shortcoming on the part of the pastor of their parish (for all men have their faults), let them not at once raise a hue and cry about him, but suffer and tolerate him, admonishing him as best they may and providing him with a decent living, lest by his poverty he be made to worry over such matters, which may hinder him in his contemplation of the Word of God.

"But as the clergy have made particular note of such passages of Scripture as favor them, setting all others aside, so we now find the laymen laying especial stress on those passages which may be construed to the injury of the former; meanwhile they are little inclined to observe those portions which speak against themselves. Faults may be found on both sides. But if the clergy begin to use the Word of God more faithfully, we may hope that in time the condition of the laity will improve, for we have the promise that the Word of God shall bear fruit where it is rightly preached. May God in His boundless mercy grant us grace to live in harmony and love, one with another. Amen.

"What has here been said has been spoken with good intent, and I hope my words will be so understood. If, however, anyone takes them in an opposite sense, be that

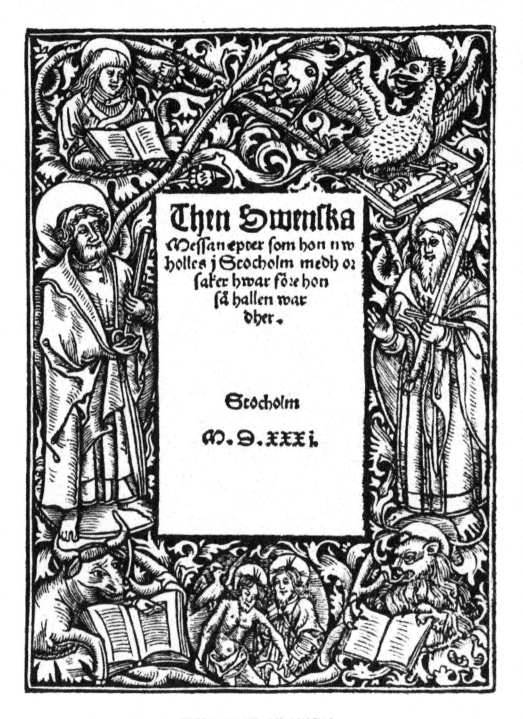

TITLE PAGE OF MISSAL.

at his own peril. I have only done my plain duty. Matt. 24: 45—51."

From the Royal Printing Office, which published all the works of Olavus Petri, was issued this same year "A Little Book on the Sacraments". While it was published anonymously, there is no doubt of Olavus Petri's authorship. He mentions but two sacraments, baptism and the Lord's Supper, and asserts here the reformatory principles embodied later in his Hand-book, i. e., Church Book, *(Een handbock påå Swensko)* and Missal *(Then Swenska Mässan)*. Immediately afterwards he published under his own name three tracts: "On Marriage" *(Een liten vnderuisning om Echteskapet)*, "On Monastic Life" *(Een liten boock j huilko closterleffwerne forclarat warder)*, and "On God's Word and Man's Decrees" *(Om gudz ordh och menniskios bodh och stadhgar)*. He pointed out, among other things, that church forms and usages, however necessary they may be, are subject to change, allowing that many old practices should be retained until the people should have been better taught, rather than to give offense to the untutored by abrupt changes.

In 1528 Olavus Petri published also "An Useful Postil" *(En nyttog postilla)*, comprising twenty-seven sermons and homilies translated from Luther's Church Postil. He explained at the outset that "many of the simple clergy have complained that they are not well able to get along with the plain gospel text alone in preaching to their congregations." This was followed in 1530 with a similar work by himself, entitled, "A Little Postil" *(Een lijten Postilla offuer all Euangelia som om söndaghanar läsen warda offuer hela året,* etc.). In his foreword the author says: "By this Postil, modest as it is, we hope to have done away with a common subterfuge, so that our church pastors will no longer be able to say that they cannot understand the text and therefore do not know what to preach. Herein the meaning is so plainly expounded that even if they simply read out of the book, it will not fail to bear fruit. For it must indeed be a very ignorant clerical, who is not able to do that much, and such an one ought by no means to hold a church pastorate."

As a specimen of Olavus Petri's preaching and his presentation of the doctrine of the sacrament of the Lord's Supper, we make these excerpts from the sermon for Palm Sunday found in his Postil:

"From the words of consecration at the institution of the Holy Communion, dear friends, it is manifest that Jesus ordained it as a sacrament, namely, that He gave us His body to eat in the form of bread, and His blood to drink in the form of wine. But His purpose in so doing we will now inquire into. We must mark, first, that after all mankind had come under the devil through sin committed by our first parents Adam and

Eve, God, our Heavenly Father, took compassion on us
and out of His mercy alone sent His Son Jesus Christ
down to us in order that He should rid us of the sins
in which we were fallen and raise us up, that we
might be made fit to reenter God's kingdom, from
which we had fallen. For this God caused Him to suffer death and to rise again from the dead. Ultimately
He made a covenant with us, that if we turn from the
devil and his ways and join the Lord, putting all our
trust in the words of Jesus Christ, spoken in behalf of
the Father, then He will be kind and merciful unto us.
The essence of this covenant is God's grace and loving-
kindness, in which we have implicit trust and faith, according to His promise, so as to follow Him in spirit.
There is nothing lacking on His part; His promise He
will surely fulfill; but on our part there is much lacking, so that we are not able to trust in His word and
promise as we ought.

"Therefore hath Christ Jesus, who was sent for our
conversion and salvation, by word and deed urgently
sought to bring us to believe and put our trust in the
promise and assurance of God. Among all his other
acts and institutions, He gave us certain tokens, which
are baptism and the sacrament of bread and wine, that
thereby we may be awakened to contemplation of the
promises and commands of God, and a realization of
our own duty, namely, to put full trust and faith in

them, to love God, who hath manifested His goodness to us out of His infinite mercy and without our merit; yea, to know and to hold Him as our gracious Father, to do His holy will, and to exercise the things signified by this sacrament. For they do not only arouse us to a steadfast faith, but also signify what shall come to pass with us. — — —

"By faith we receive all the benefits promised us in God's covenant, not for the sake of the act by which we are baptized or receive the body and blood of Christ, but by faith, which accompanies the act and through which we receive the Holy Spirit, who worketh all these things. Yet, as this is wrought through outward and bodily words and sacramental means, the Scriptures in various places attribute it to the Word and the sacraments, speaking of the Word as the word of life and of the physical administration of baptism as the new birth, although the new birth is the work of the Holy Spirit alone. Thus we see the fruit and use of this sacrament, namely, that it revives our faith, on which depends our salvation. For by faith we become the children of God, and His heirs, the brothers of Christ and joint heirs with Him, and become so closely united with Christ as to be of one body with Him and with all those who constitute His Church, that is, the communion of saints. This is also expressed in the words of the Apostle Paul (1 Cor. 10: 17), that we are all one bread, one body: for we all partake of the one bread. And as we become one with Christ, so we surely shall remain with Him in eternity. Inasmuch as this sacrament is received unto the forgiveness of sins and justification before God, it is rightly used by those who, feeling oppressed by their sins, earnestly desire to be rid of them; who hunger and thirst for righteousness, though weak in the faith through which they are to receive all these things. Hence this sacrament is of great use to them. Yea, to them alone, but not to them that falsely rely on their own righteousness and freedom from sin; for the latter do not hunger and thirst for righteousness and forgiveness, the which they claim to have already received. From this it doth appear that it is wrong to compel people, by rules and statutes, to go to the Lord's table, whether or not they have this hunger. Let it also be remarked that manifest sinners and such as will not abandon their evil ways should not be suffered to partake of this sacrament, inasmuch as they are not moved thereto by the aforesaid hunger for righteousness and the forgiveness of sin, seeing that they still hold fast to a life of sin.— — —"

Appended to the postil was the Catechism of Olavus Petri, which, like Luther's larger catechism, was designed as an aid to the clergy in religious instruction. While following Luther in the main, he writes independently, his explanations of the Lord's Prayer being entirely original, each in the form of a short and beautifully worded prayer. In this connection may be mentioned a book published by him in 1529, bearing the title: "A Little Introduction into the Holy Scriptures" (*En liten ingong i then helga schrifft*). This valuable work was translated from a "Manual for Young Christians," written by J. TOLTS, a German Lutheran pastor.

The Church Book of Olavus Petri was issued in 1529 in consequence of the transactions of the Church Council of Örebro, held the same year. The Church Book contains rituals for baptism, marriage, the churching of mothers, visits to the sick, consecrating a marriage after death, burial, and the preparation of convicts for execution. It corresponds to the Catholic Manuale with the exclusion of purely Roman Catholic forms, such as masses for the dead. This was the first Protestant Church Book not only of the Church of Sweden but of the entire Protestant Church, Luther's baptismal formulary of 1523 being the only Protestant form for church rites published up to this time.

It may be stated here that many precious jewels from this "Hand-book" have been preserved in the Swedish Lutheran Church Books. Among these may be mentioned the beautiful prayer composed by Olavus Petri to be read at burial of the dead, beginning, "Almighty, merciful and eternal God, who on account of sin," etc. This prayer has been translated from the Swedish Church Book of 1811 and inserted in the Prussian "Hofkirchen Agende" of 1822. The same is true of the Swedish order requiring the minister to throw earth into the grave three times, while he says: "Dust thou art; unto dust shalt thou return; Jesus Christ, our Saviour, shall raise thee on the last day." This form was translated from the Hand-book of Olavus Petri for the Malmö Church Book of 1532 for Skåne, for the Danish ritual of 1680, for the Prussian Agenda, and for the Bavarian Agenda of 1850.

That several of these formulas had been written some time before appears from the Rhymed Chronicle of Messenius, which has this passage:

> "On Master Olov's wedding day
> The Lutherans their respects did pay
> By holding their first Swedish mass,
> The which is plain to every class;
> In Wittenberg this happened too,
> And Master Olov was there to view,
> When at Carlstadt's wedding feast
> A German mass was said by a Priest."

(The English is purposely made crude in imitation of the original, which runs thus:

> *På Mäster Oluffs Bröllopsdag*
> *War Lutherskom så till behag,*
> *Att första Swenska Mässa tå*
> *Blef hållen, then alla förstå,*

Mäster Oluff hade så sedt
I Wittenberg förr wara skedt
På Carolstadii Bröllops fest
Ther hölt först Tysk mässa en Präst.")

"The Reason Why the Mass Should Be in Swedish" *(Orsack hvar före Messan böör wara på thet tungomål som then menighe man forstondelighit är)* was published by Olavus Petri in 1531, in defense of his simultaneous work, "The Swedish Mass" *(Then Swenska Messan epter som hon nw holles i Stockolm medh orsaker hwar före hon så hållen wardher).*

Modeling upon Luther's "The German Mass" of 1526, he recast the Catholic Mass in an evangelical and critical spirit, while the Confession of Sins (I, poor, sinful man," etc.) is entirely his own work. The revised editions of 1535 and 1537 were issued by the author himself; that of 1541 by GEORG NORMAN.

"A Little Book in which is Explained How Man Gains Eternal Salvation" was published by Olavus Petri in 1535. Its complete agreement with Luther's theology and the Pauline doctrines has been pointed out in the foregoing sketch of Olavus Petri at Wittenberg.

We make the following typical extracts from this work:

"In His infinite mercy God sent Jesus Christ into this world in order that He should be a Mediator between God, who was wroth, and man, who had offended Him, and by His suffering and death to render satisfaction for their sins. When all this was finished, He sent His apostles out into the world to make known to all men that God, who was angered by the sins of men, had now been propitiated through the suffering and death of Christ. To all those who would now follow Christ, put their faith and trust in Him, and receive baptism and be taught Christianity, all would be forgiven, so that they would find favor with God and receive eternal salvation. If they were to receive the precious treasure procured by Christ, therefore, it must be accomplished through faith. For this reason Paul took such pains to make it clear to all that righteousness comes not from works but from faith in Jesus Christ unto all that believe. He also presents many examples in proof thereof. — — —

"Now righteousness and the forgiveness of sins are the same thing. But forgiveness of sin we receive through faith in Jesus Christ, and trust in Him, hence righteousness results from faith in Christ, for Jesus Christ alone of all men was without sin, righteous and good. In Him there was nothing to displease God; so good and righteous was He that to those who have communion with Him all is forgiven when they come before God, and they are for the same reason like Christ in God's sight, although in themselves great and grievous sinners. Now it can no longer be laid against them that they themselves are sinners, for God, who alone has power to punish sin, forgives their sins and looks upon them as good and righteous men. Sinners alone oppose God and His commandments. Who is there now to accuse man on account of his sins, when He who was wroth condemns not, but rather justifies (Rom. 8). We need not now fear our accusers; but when sin and the devil would terrify us by pointing to all our evil deeds, we can answer and say: 'Depart, Satan! Thou hast no concern with these things. Inasmuch as God, against whom I have trespassed, is propitiated and has forgiven me all my transgressions, thou hast nothing to do with this matter.'

"Christ, as we have said, is the one man who is without sin and in whom is all righteounsess, yea, all sin and unrighteousness disappears in Him, so that where He is, there no sin can be found; He is that Lamb of God, which taketh away the sins of the world. He who has Him has with Him all righteousness and the forgiveness of sins. But Him we can have only through faith, and in order that we may have occasion and opportunity to receive Him, the Word and the sacraments have been given, whereby He is offered unto us. When we receive the Word and the sacraments, putting our faith and trust in them, then we have Christ; and having Him, we have forgiveness and righteousness through Him.

"God has promised that he who believes in Christ shall for His sake be accounted righteous. But the promise of God requires faith, and if we have faith in it, we have righteousness through Christ, who was promised; thus righteousness comes from faith, not that righteousness which we earn by our own works, but that which we receive through Christ. We are held devout and good and the friends of God for His sake, not for our own sake. We receive; we do not give. We stand without sin before God, because He forgave all our sins, not because we ourselves have rendered satisfaction. This Paul proves with the words of David: Blessed is he whose transgression is forgiven, whose sin is covered, and to whom iniquity is not imputed (Ps. 32: 1, 2). In these words David clearly says that salvation and the forgiveness of sins, that is, righteousness, comes from God's forgiveness of our transgressions, not from any reparation on our part, for if we could propitiate God, no forgiveness would be needed.

"But where there is to be faith, there the Word of God must go before, as the foundation for faith; therefore a faith not resting on God's Word is not acceptable to Him. It is not possible that faith unto righteousness could have any other foundation than the Word of God, through which man receives sure and perfect knowledge of God's disposition toward man. Where there is any other foundation than the Word of God, surely there is no true faith."

"Swedish Songs and Hymns" *(Swenske songer eller wisor nw på nytt prentade, forokade och under en annan skick än tillförenna utsatte)* is a work founded on two previous collections of hymns published by Olavus Petri. Of the first, that of 1526, no copy has been preserved. It contains ten hymns, including the one still in use in almost literal form as number 49 in the Swedish Psalm Book. The version here quoted is from the Hymnal (No. 5):

Thou, Jesus Christ, didst man become
   From death us to deliver;
Thy pitying eye beheld our doom,
   That we were lost forever;
Thou gavest hope in direst need,
When death and hell with gaping greed
   Were ready to devour us.

Thou couldst not bear that Satan's might
   Had in its grasp enslaved us;
In pity Thou didst for us fight,
   And hast in mercy saved us.
From heaven Thou cam'st for our release,
To purchase our eternal peace
   By bitter death and suffering.

And Thou hast taught us in Thy Word
   That faith shall life inherit,

For Thou art merciful, O Lord,
  And sav'st us by Thy merit,
If we but simply do believe
That all Thy children shall receive
  The blessings Thou hast promised.

Our brother Thou art now become —
  An honor beyond measure!
Thou wouldst our life with mercy crown
  And give us richest treasure.
The world's contempt we need not fear,
God's Son is now our brother dear:
  What power can now destroy us?

All praise to Thee eternally,
  For all Thy gracious favor;
We are God's children now with Thee,
  Lord Jesus Christ our Saviour.
Well may we one and all rejoice,
And praise our God with heart and voice;
  He is our gracious Father.

(Rendered into English by G. H. Trabert.)

From the second collection, that of 1530, two hymns by Olavus Petri are still in use, namely, the one just quoted and No. 21 in the same book. A third one attributed to Olavus Petri (No. 59) has now no resemblance to his Christmas hymn beyond the first line. No. 21 of the present Psalm Book, slightly altered from the author's version, is thus rendered in the Hymnal (No. 118):

Our Father, merciful and good,
   Who dost to Thee invite us,
O cleanse us in the Saviour's blood,
   And to Thyself unite us.
Send unto us Thy holy Word,
   And let it guide us ever;
Then in this world of darkness, Lord,
   Shall naught from Thee us sever:
   Grant us, O Lord, this favor!

O God and man, Christ Jesus blest!
   Our sorrows Thou didst carry.
Our wants and cares Thou knowest best,
   For Thou with us didst tarry.
O Jesus Christ, our Brother dear,
   To us and every nation
Thy spirit send, let Him draw near
   With truth and consolation,
   That we may see salvation.

We cry to Thee with one accord,
   'Tis all that can avail us;
For none doth hear and keep Thy Word,
   If, Lord, Thy grace doth fail us.
Consider then, we humbly pray,
   For our dear Saviour's merit,
How Satan soweth tares alway,
   And send, O Lord, Thy Spirit,
   That we may life inherit.

Come, Holy Ghost, Thy grace impart,
   Tear Satan's snares asunder.

The Word of God keep in our heart,
    And lead us safely yonder;
Then, sanctified, for evermore,
    In Christ alone confiding,
We'll sing His praise and Him adore,
    His precious Word us guiding
    To heavenly joys abiding.

(Rendered into English by Augustus Nelson.)

Of the last named edition there is now in existence only a fragmentary copy containing ten hymns, four being written by Olavus Petri himself. The Psalm Book of 1536 contained four additional hymns from his pen, the others being translations or elaborations of old Latin hymns or German Reformation songs. One example from this edition is No. 46 in the present hymnody of the Church of Sweden. The corresponding hymn by Luther contains ten stanzas, Olavus Petri having left out stanzas 7, 8, and 10, and added one of his own, the triumphant closing stanza of the Swedish hymn:

We thank Thee, Lord, for boundless grace,
    And sing Thy praise forever,
For granting us in dire distress
    Thine everlasting favor.
Both death and hell were stricken down,
When Thou didst for our sins atone,
    O Jesus, blessed Saviour.

(Rendered into English by Ernst W. Olson.)

This hymn has since undergone many successive revisions until in its present form it became one of the grandest hymns of the Lutheran Church. All but one of the original hymns by Olavus Petri in the edition of 1536 are still retained in the Swedish Psalm Book of 1695 and 1819. In the so-called "Wallinian Psalm Book" of the latter year there are twenty-two hymns from the Psalm Book of Olavus Petri (1530 edition), but many more ought to have been included, especially his excellent Reformation hymn, "Thy Sacred Word, O Lord, of old" *(O Herre Gud, ditt helga ord)*. This hymn is taken up again in revised form in most of the newly proposed Swedish hymnodies. Seven of the nine stanzas are here reproduced in English according to the original form of the hymn, successive alterations and revisions being disregarded in the interest of authenticity.

> Thy sacred Word, O Lord, of old
>   Was veiled about and darkened,
> And in its stead were legends told,
>   To which the people harkened;
> Thy Word, for which the faithful yearned,
>   The worldlings kept in hiding,
> And into human fables turned
>   Thy truth, the all-abiding.
>
> Thy Word is the true bread of life
>   To hungering souls and humble.
> Who seek their all by worldly strife
>   In worldly snares shall stumble.

Jesus·

Thet Nyia Testamen=
tit på Swensko·

TITLE PAGE OF NEW TESTAMENT OF 1526.

The welfare of their souls but ill
   They serve who leave the Master,
Deserting His true fold at will,
   In quest of other pasture.

All planting not ordained by God
   Forthwith shall be uprooted;
That growth encumbers but the sod
   Which to no use is suited.
God's Word shall stand forevermore,
   A safe and sure foundation;
Who builds on it shall live secure
   Through storm and tribulation.

Now thanks and praise be to our Lord,
   Who boundless grace bestoweth,
And daily through the sacred Word
   His precious gifts forthshoweth.
His Word is come to light again,
   A trusty lamp to guide us;
No strange and divers teachings then
   Shall wilder and divide us.

So let us wander in His light
   Through whom the light was given,
That we may always walk aright
   And find the path to heaven.
To traps and snares he falls a prey
   Who walks in darksome places,
While on the straight and narrow way
   Shine all the heavenly graces.

Though heaven's high tent shall be uprolled,
　　And earthly things shall vanish,
God's Word, by holy men enscrolled,
　　No power can hide or banish.
By whatsoever evil thing
　　My soul be overtaken,
To Thee forever will I cling,
　　Eternal Rock unshaken.

Now I beseech Thee, Father dear,
　　To grant that I may cherish
Within my heart that faith sincere
　　Which shall not change or perish;
Then shall my soul depart in peace,
　　When called from life's contentions,
To dwell with Thee without surcease
　　In heaven's eternal mansions.

(Rendered into English by Ernst W. Olson.)

In 1535 Olavus Petri issued his "Admonition to All Evangelical Preachers throughout Sweden" *(Förmaning til alla Euangeliska Predicare öffuer heela Swerige, ther hwar och een Christtrogen Menniskia må haffua rettelse utaff, huru hon sigh skicka skal, tå Förfölielse påkommer för Gudz Ord skull).* In this exposition of the tenth chapter of Matthew, dedicated to his brother clergymen, he admonishes them to have firm faith in the rightfulness and complete Scripturalness of the evangelical cause, despite all difficulties. His work closes with these words: "From peace and too much tranquillity we grow negligent and become less attentive to the duty of our office than in time of persecution. May God give us His Holy Spirit, to awaken us and make us all diligent in time of peace and of strife."

Among the later writings of Olavus Petri is his valuable "Swedish Chronicle," a critical work which incurred the displeasure of King Gustav I. and was accordingly suppressed. The king also took offense at his published sermon of 1539, "Against the Horrible Oaths and Blasphemies Now Generally Used."

His "Rules for Judges," already mentioned, and his "Sermon on the Age and Early Mutations of the World," together with his drama, "The Comedy of Tobias," printed in 1550, were his last literary works. His latter years Olavus Petri gave undivided to his divine and richly blest calling as a preacher and pastor.

Laurentius Andreæ is better known as a church politician than as an evangelical minister. As a writer and church reformer he is most familiar to us through his official writings in the capacity of secretary to the king. Aside from these, we have but one small tract from his hand, "A Short Instruction on Faith and Good Works," published in 1528. It is clear and simple in style, but deals largely in the generalities of Christian doctrine. A quotation reads: "Good works do not make men good; on the contrary, good men do good works."

After Laurentius Petri had been made archbishop in 1531, he published, in collaboration with Olavus Petri and possibly others, the Swedish Bible, under the title, *Biblia, Thet är all then Helga Scrifft på Swensko.* It was printed in 1540—41, at Uppsala. The translation conformed more closely to Luther's translation than had the Swedish version of the New Testament by Olavus Petri, published in 1526.

In 1555 Laurentius Petri published a voluminous Postil, the bulk of which is made up of sermons rendered from the German. In 1553 he had issued a new edition of the Psalm Book, and in 1567 he published the Swedish Psalm Book under the title: *Then Swenska Psalmeboken förbättrat och medh flere Songer förmerat och Kalendarium.* This revised edition contained thirty-nine new hymns, most of them written or translated by Olavus Petri, including nos. 16, 24, 134, and 194 in the book now in use.

In the early part of his reign, ERIC XIV. had leanings toward Calvinism. This caused Laurentius Petri to publish, in 1562, a polemical work in dialogue form entitled, "On Sundry Points Relating to the Holy Supper of Our Lord Jesus Christ" *(Om någor stycker wårs Herras Jesu Christi Nattvard anrörandes).* Under King JOHN III., who inclined to Romanism, the aged archbishop in 1571 published "The Swedish Church Service" *(Then Swenska Kyrkeordningen).*

This work was the first compendium of evangelical ordinances, acquiring added significance as a book of
service and a manual in pastoral work. Its first article,
treating of the sermon and of Christian teaching, contains this pronouncement, most true and ever worthy of
note: "Hence we gather that to preach the gospel is
nothing else but to preach the forgiveness of sin, not in
any other name whatsoever (as has been done under the
popes), but in the name of Jesus Christ alone, who is
dead and risen for us; and further, that we are each
and all to preach repentance."

III. THE REFORMATION OF THE CHURCH IN SWEDEN

THE reformation of the Church in Sweden was undertaken by Olavus Petri, not only by means of oral preaching, but in great measure by writing and publishing, as here shown. But not all members of the Church could be reached—not even with the Swedish version of the Bible. This was true especially in regard to the rank and file of the people, who, themselves unable to read, were at that time led and controlled by rebellious monks and prelates. The populace, therefore, naturally held fast to the traditional church usages and insisted on the continued maintenance of the convents and other church institutions. This being the situation, the aid of King Gustav I. was both needful and in several respects valuable to the Swedish reformers. Incited by their Roman Catholic priests and by their hatred for "the treacherous Sture," the Dalecarlians set up the demand "that no new faith or Lutherism *(lutheri)* should be forced upon them, and that the king ought to "burn or put to death by other means all those who ate meat on Friday or Saturday." Gustav Vasa, however, proceeded without fear to further and establish the Reformation in his realm.

To the national diet known as the Riksdag of Väster-ås, convoked by the king for June 16, 1527, the four estates—nobles, clergy, bourgeoisie, and peasants—assembled in large numbers. As chancellor to the king, Laurentius Andreæ read the royal "Propositions" to the Riksdag, from which we quote:

"A great outcry against His Grace has also been raised, alleging that he fleeces the churches and cloisters; likewise that he has brought in a new religion." In answer, the Propositions set up the new principle that the wealth of the churches and cloisters was the property of the people, which, as such, was at the disposal of the king and his council, acting on behalf of the people."

We quote further: "His grace knows full well that he is causing to be preached the pure Word and gospel of God, as the Lord himself hath commanded.— Furthermore, His Grace hath called hither a number of those who so preach, and they are now present." The king requested that the debate be carried on "in the presence of you all, to the end that the party which is in the right may be in power, supported by all, and thereby all such strife be ended."

The revenues of the state had been greatly reduced

by intermittent revolts and by the constant encroach-
ments of the Church on state and private property.
Therefore the king demanded that the castles of the
bishops and all other superfluous property and income
of the Church should be turned over to the state. If
this were not done, said the king, it was his purpose to
lay down the scepter, and in that event he urged the
assembly to cast about for another ruler "more gentle
and successful."

The bourgeoisie (representatives of the cities and
the mining industries) ultimately declared their readi-
ness to live and die with the king. As to the "new
faith," they "demanded to know, before they adjourned,
which party was in the right, declaring their willingness
to listen to a disputation on that point, and urged that
the true doctrine thus established should be preached
everywhere. The spokesmen for the peasantry, while
assuring the king of their loyalty, also requested a discussion on matters of faith, but evaded by subterfuges
the demand of the king for binding promises. The nobility gave a different answer. They pledged loyalty to
the king and support to his reforms and demanded "that
the pure Word of God be preached everywhere, according to God's command, not uncertain signs, man-made
legends and fables, as has been very generally practiced
heretofore." The estates ultimately joined in the resolutions of the nobility, in order to induce the king to

withdraw his abdication and resume the government. Although the bishops did not take direct part in the framing of the resolutions of the Diet, yet these prelates were obliged to submit, and they finally declared themselves satisfied, "however rich or poor His Grace designed to make them."

The resolutions and acts passed and ratified at the Riksdag of Västerås are found recorded, partly in "The Västerås Recess," partly in the "Ordinantia." In the Recess, the states-general pledge loyalty to the king and favor increased revenues for the crown and betterment of the economic condition of the nobility through the restoration to them of certain landed estates which had come into the possession of the Church. The representatives pray also, "that the Word of God be preached in its purity throughout the kingdom."

The Ordinantia, the contents of which are formulated in Twenty Articles, establishes the principle that the king is the temporal head of the Church, and that the clergy are the equals of the laymen before the law. After the passage of the acts, but prior to the ratification of the Recess, the disputation between the adherents of the old and new order took place at the request of the states-general. The leading parts were taken by the two antagonists, Peder Galle and Olavus Petri. The principal subjects discussed were, the false indulgences of the pope, the secular power of the bishops, and the laws and ordinances of the Church. At the close of the debate, the representatives expressed their approval of the arguments presented by Olavus Petri, and when the acts of the Diet had been formally ratified, the king consented to resume the reins of government.

By the ratification of the Recess and the Ordinantia, the Church of Sweden declared its independence of the pope, but it was made a State Church, directly under the jurisdiction of the king. The Holy Scriptures were declared the supreme norm of faith. The bishops were compelled to give up their castles and estates. Monks and nuns left the reduced convents, several friars going to Lapland as missionaries.

At the time of the Uppsala Council in 1593, and for a short time thereafter, Vadstena Cloister was the only remaining monastery. Bishop Hans Brask, the leading figure among the Romanists, soon left the country of his fathers to go into voluntary exile. Bishop MAGNUS SOMMAR of Strängnäs and MAGNUS HARALDSON of Skara, both elected in 1522 but not yet consecrated, in the fall of 1527 were given the choice of submitting to consecration without the pope's sanction or vacating their offices. Together with Bishop MÅRTEN SKYTTE of Åbo they were subsequently so consecrated in 1528, at Strängnäs, by Petrus Magni, bishop of Västerås, himself consecrated by the pope at Rome. One week later, these bishops officiated at the coronation of Gustav Vasa at Uppsala, when Olavus Petri preached his noted Coronation Sermon.

Shortly after the coronation, the king convoked a council of the bishops and other prominent members of the clergy to sit at Örebro in February, 1529, for the purpose of establishing a liturgy for the Church in accordance with the Holy Scriptures. One reason for the convocation was that one MELCHIOR HOFFMAN, a German cooper, had come to Stockholm in 1526, provided with recommendations from Luther and BUGENHAGEN, and begun to preach apocalyptic and iconoclastic sermons. Compelled to leave Sweden the following year, Hoffman went to Holstein and thence to Wittenberg. Then Luther learnt to know the man better, whereupon he recalled his recommendation and warned the people of Bremen against him. Subsequently Hoffman accepted ZWINGLI's doctrine of the Eucharist, next going over to the Anabaptists, and dying in prison at Strassburg in 1543. It was the appearance of this Melchior Hoffman in Stockholm which gave rise to the story of alleged Anabaptist excesses in that city in 1524, supposed to have been led by Melchior Rink and Knipperdolling. This tradition has been passed down from the Chronicle of PEDER SVART, bishop of Västerås, to the works of Bishop C. A. CORNELIUS, although it was subjected to doubt in Archbishop H. REUTERDAHL's History of the Reformation. Neither Olavus Petri, nor the opponents of the Reformation, Peter Galle, Paul Heliæ, and Hans Brask, made mention of any such Anabaptist activities in Stockholm in 1524 or 1525. In *Kyrklig Tidskrift,* 1896, Dean HERMAN LUND-STRÖM, after making thorough research, disposed of the story as a pure fabrication.

The Council of Örebro passed resolutions accentuating the necessity of preaching the Word of God in its clearness and purity; in other respects its proceedings made a compromise between the old and the new order regarding church ceremonies and practices. This was due partly to the conditions of the time, partly to the wish of the king that the people be first instructed and the reformation of the church order be undertaken in the second place. On the one hand, the German Lutherans in Stockholm, with their pastor, one TILEMAN, took offense at this; on the other, the Romanists in the country were further embittered and renewed their plottings. Bishop Magnus of Skara, with TURE JÖNS-SON, judge of the district of Västergötland, and others, first fomented a revolt in the northern part of the province of Småland, against Gustav Vasa, whom they called "the heretical king;" but when the peasantry of Västergötland, met on the heath of Larf, refused to make common cause with them, the revolt subsided, whereupon Bishop Magnus and Ture Jönsson left Sweden. The Dalecarlians subsequently rose against the king for the third time. This was known as the Bell Revolt, having its cause in the opposition to an order of the government that each church was to yield up one church bell or its equivalent in money to help pay the government debt to Lübeck. This revolt also was of short duration, the Dalecarlians soon regretting their hasty act.

After Johannes Magnus had left Sweden, the Church was without an archbishop until Laurentius Petri, the younger brother of Olavus Petri, was invested with that office, with the king's sanction. This man was an almost unknown schoolmaster in Uppsala, whose gentle manner and conversation gained him favor with the king. A life guard of fifty men placed at his disposal by the monarch he soon discharged as needless, and the appropriation for their keep he afterwards used for the support of fifty poor students. Laurentius Andreæ, the king's chancellor, was soon discharged, and Olavus Petri, who succeeded to the office, remained only until 1533, when he, too, was discharged.

The cause for the king's dissatisfaction with these, the earliest Swedish reformers, was to be found in their opposition to his increasingly autocratic tendencies. Andreæ firmly maintained the independence of the Church alongside of the state, and Olavus Petri held that the supreme duty of kings is to further the Christian and moral advancement of their peoples and that they must bow to the ordinances of God, even as their humblest subjects. The combined interests of Church and state had more or less predisposed Gustav Vasa for the Evangelical Reformation from the very beginning of his reign, and later this tendency developed and ambition on his part to become the sole ruler of both Church and state. This is clearly apparent from his letter to the people of the province of Uppland, assembled at a provincial fair in 1539. The king wrote:

"Let every one of you look after your horses, fields, meadows, wives, children, and cattle, and refrain from setting before us a goal for our government or religion; for it behooves us, in behalf of God and justice and for purely natural reasons, as a Christian king on this earth to dictate rules and decrees for you and for all our subjects; and it is meet that you, if you would escape our wrath and severe punishment, remain obedient to our royal commands, both in worldly things and in religious matters."

The politico-ecclesiastical policies of the king were furthered and shaped to a degree by two Germans, who soon after their arrival gained the confidence of Gustav. One of these was CONRAD VON PYHY, alias PEUTINGER, who arrived in 1538. This adventurer was made chancellor to the king the same year, and in that capacity he sought to organize the Church of Sweden after German and English models. The second adviser was a Pomeranian nobleman named GEORG NORMAN, a Master of Arts of the University of Wittenberg. He came to Sweden in 1539 and in the same year was appointed *"ordinator* and *superattendent."* As such he was vested with power to exercise royal jurisdiction over "bishops, prelates, and all divines" of the Swedish Church, and to appoint and discharge "all divines and preachers."

Gustav had taken offense at the "Swedish Chronicle" of Olavus Petri, a critical patriotic work, and his royal mind was further embittered by that patriot's "Sermon against the Horrible Oaths." Olavus Petri was also said to have joined with Laurentius Andreæ in censuring the king for encroachment on the freedom of the Church, especially through the autocracy exercised by Norman with his consent. This criticism of the king's policy, together with the plottings of Von Pyhy and the opponents of the Evangelical Reformation, combined to bring about the sad catastrophe at the Diet of Örebro, at Christmas, 1539, when Olavus Petri and Andreæ were arrested on the charge of lese majesty. On New Year's Eve they were summoned before a court of fifteen judges, divine and secular, including Von Pyhy, Norman and Laurentius Petri. It is more than likely that Von Pyhy had assisted the enraged king in framing the charges, which were comprised in a lengthy document, a hodgepodge of heinous charges interspersed with passages from Scripture.

One of the charges against Andreæ was his alleged claim that with his evangelical flock of followers he was as powerful as the king; another, that he had asked the king what he wanted with so much money, since good friends would be better and more useful to His Grace than large sums of money. Further, the two Reformers were charged with having induced the king to favor the Reformation of the Church, a step which had caused His Grace great worry and sacrifice, and brought on revolts. The gravest charge, however, was that by way of the confessional the two churchmen had been cognizant of a conspiracy of the Lübeckers, detected in 1536, against the life of the king, but had failed to inform him of the plot. Of this the king, however, had been aware for some time and had spoken to Andreæ about the matter, it was claimed.

Olavus Petri replied in defense that he had always stood by the king and had never sought to injure him. Andreæ requested a transcript of the numerous written accusations in order to submit his defense in writing. This was refused him, it is alleged. On the second of January, 1540, the second day of the trial, the defendants were condemned to die by the sword, on the alleged ground that "Master Olov, without pain and torture," had admitted that he knew of the plot and

MONUMENT TO OLAVUS PETRI, ERECTED IN STOCKHOLM, 1898.

yet kept his silence, having only conferred with Master
Lars. The court, however, sent a deputation to the
king with a request that the lives of the convicted men
be spared; and doubtless the king's purpose was, not to
execute the Reformers, but to set at nought their power.

In his memorial work of 1893, "On the Reformation
of the Church in Sweden," Archbishop A. N. SUND-
BERG has this to say of the verdict passed on Olavus
Petri and Laurentius Andreæ:

"Both of these great men, as is well known, were at
that time charged with high treason and condemned to
death by a very peculiarly constituted court and on the
most wretched evidence."

The sentences were commuted from death to heavy
fines, which reduced Andreæ to poverty, and he died in
want in 1552. The bourgeoisie of Stockholm paid the
fine for Olavus Petri, and the king subsequently was
favorably disposed toward him, partly to requite him
for the injustice inflicted, partly to gain him for his
private ends. Thus Olavus Petri, who had been ordained to the holy ministry in 1539, was then appointed
inspector of the Stockholm school and the year after was
made rector of Storkyrkan in Stockholm.

He was requested by the king to write the chronicles
of his reign, the monarch himself outlining the plan of
the work. A few years later the king asked him to
write a history of Christian the Tyrant and his reign.

On this point Prof. Schück in his valuable work on Olavus Petri says:

"So far as known, the king failed in his attempts to make an official historian out of the former oppositionist. In his sermons, too, Olavus Petri appears to have spoken his mind as fearlessly as before."

So dear to Olavus Petri were truth, liberty, and the gospel of Christ, that he could not become the official flatterer of Gustav Vasa. That role fell to Bishop Peder Svart, in his chronicle, which closes with the year 1533.

Georg Norman and his co-workers sought in vain to reconstruct the church government arbitrarily to suit the king. They patterned after the Church in Germany by abolishing the episcopate and substituting seniors, etc. With the aid of the German counselor and his assistants, the king had better success in his efforts to rifle the churches, to make the clergy over into clerks in the pay of the government, to strip the gold and silver from ecclesiastical vestments, all of which led to the dangerous revolt of 1542—43, known as the Dacke Feud. Even afterwards, the king continued to pillage the property of the Church, but from that time on he proceeded with greater caution.

Von Pyhy fell into disfavor with the king and died in prison. Norman was deprived of the superintendency of the Church, but remained until his death in

1553 the chief counselor of the king in all church and state affairs.

The wealth gathered in from the churches more than sufficed for the expenditures of the realm, and the surplus flowed into the private coffers of the king. Queen MARGARETA is said to have made clothes for her children out of chasubles, and used altar cloths for pillow covers in the royal castles. On the other hand, very little was done for the promotion of learning and for the education of able ministers of the gospel. Nothing was done to rehabilitate the University of Uppsala. The king appropriated the revenues from sundry small prebendary pastorates for the maintenance of a few students at the German universities of Rostock and Wittenberg, and he urged the people to send their sons to these schools.

The last six years of the reign of Gustav I. proved peaceful and prosperous, and were especially favorable to the industries and commerce of Sweden. He is rightly considered the organizer of the Swedish state and its institutions. He died September 29, 1560, having three months before bidden a touching farwell to the assembled members of the Riksdag. In his farewell address the king uttered this testimony: "Comfort and blessing have come to me and to you in rich measure through the true knowledge of the Word of God."

Olavus Petri somewhere has said: "It is no great task

to punish and to break down—that a heathen or a Turk can do; it is a greater thing to strike down evil and with reason and understanding set up and establish that which is right and true." As a reformer he did break down that part of the power and intrenchments of the Roman Catholic Church which was foredoomed to destruction; but his greatness lies in the upbuilding of the Church of Sweden on a firm evangelical foundation. This was accomplished primarily through his translation of the New Testament into the Swedish tongue and through his part in the translation of the entire Bible. His "Book of Service," "The Swedish Mass," and Psalm Book constituted in fact the popular evangelical Lutheran confession in the reign of Gustav I., before the Church of Sweden had been prepared for the direct adoption of any official Lutheran confession, not even that of Augsburg, adopted in 1530. The reformatory resolution passed at Västerås in 1527 was simply this, "that the Word of God be preached clearly and purely throughout the kingdom." The states-general declared that those accused of a new and false doctrine "had good ground and did not preach anything but the Word of God."

True, the general spiritual culture was still low, and worldliness seemed to prevail everywhere, yet the Word preached by the Reformers and their followers was not in vain, but bore fruit according to God's promise, being in truth the Word that giveth life. This fruitage was apparent during the trying period up to 1573, when that patient but staunch Lutheran, Laurentius Petri, occupied the archiepiscopal chair, and more especially in the Decree of the Uppsala Council in 1593. Then and there the unaltered Augsburg Confession was unanimously adopted. Following that significant act, Professsor NIKOLAUS BOTNIENSIS, presiding at the Council, made the memorable declaration: "Now is Sweden become as one man, and we all have one Lord and God." The truth of his words was subsequently proved in the war waged by GUSTAV II. ADOLF in defense of the Protestant cause.

As rector of Storkyrkan in Stockholm, Olavus Petri until his death faithfully continued his pastoral work, preaching the gospel of Christ earnestly, clearly, and in its unadulterated purity. Possibly the work of his last years was carried on with some degree of disappointment, there being no signs of any great general revival for repentance and faith among his beloved countrymen. A letter from Bishop MICHAEL AGRICOLA, the church reformer of Finland, to AMUND LORENTZEN, a Stockholm publisher, written about a year before Olavus Petri died, throws light on this period of his life. It tells of the difficult and oppressive conditions under which the Finnish Reformation was carried out and further affords a glimpse of the high popular respect in which Olavus Petri was held in the sister country. Agricola wrote:

"Hunger is every man's guest among the peasantry as also among the clergy. In the cities neither grain nor salt is to be had. This wretched poverty you ought to make known to Master Olavus Petri. Maybe his fatherly compassion will find some remedy, with the grace of God, such as preaching from his pulpit on the vengeance, plague, and punishment of God on this poor land, whereby he might induce the nobility, the bourgeoisie, and any other godly people to send us some help in the form of grain at the first open water." Finland did receive the aid asked for, undoubtedly through the petitions and exhortations of Olavus Petri.

The Swedish Reformer sometimes has been compared to his teacher Martin Luther. The two men were indeed very much alike, particularly in their firm but humble trust in the Word of God and its promises. Yet Olavus Petri was not a mere imitator of Luther. The cordiality and good humor found in the great German Reformer is lacking in his Swedish counterpart. The language of the latter is characterized by greater terseness and austerity. Olavus Petri was also a historian, endowed with the critical faculty, and as such he knew how to make historical applications to current conditions.

Olavus Petri passed away April 19, 1552, five days

after the death of his co-worker Laurentius Andreæ.
The great Swedish Church Reformer went peacefully
to sleep "after having made an edifying Christian preparation and an express confession of his faith in Christ
Jesus." His remains were buried in Stockholm, close
to the pulpit from which he had so often preached.
Blessed be his memory, and God be thanked for the
work of this His servant!

At the joint commemoration at Uppsala, in 1893, of
the Uppsala Council of 1593 and of the birth of Olavus
Petri one hundred years before, it was resolved to erect
a monument to that foremost Church Reformer of
Sweden, and in 1898 a statue of Olavus Petri was
placed in front of Storkyrkan in Stockholm. It was
unveiled on September thirtieth, with imposing ceremonies, in the presence of the royal family, representatives of the Church in council assembled, and a large
multitude. On the pedestal are inscribed these words
from the introduction to "The Swedish Mass":

"WE SWEDES ALSO BELONG TO GOD,
AS WELL AS OTHER PEOPLE,
AND THE TONGUE WE SPEAK,
THAT GOD HATH GIVEN US."

The works of Olavus Petri were republished, 1914—
17, in an edition de luxe of four large volumes, by the
Swedish Students' Christian Movement, the text being
reproduced literatim and edited by Professor BENGT

HESSELMAN, while Dr. K. B. WESTMAN furnished excellent historical introductions to the volumes. One highly competent reviewer has said of this publication: "It is at once a patriotic and a churchly enterprise of the greatest importance to the Swedish Church and the Swedish people." At the quadricentennial Reformation Jubilee celebrated at Uppsala October thirty-first, 1917, the degree of Doctor of Theology (D. D.) was conferred on Professor Henrik Schück, rector of the university, by Archbishop NATHAN SÖDERBLOM, with the specific announcement that this was done in grateful recognition of Professor Schück's noteworthy services in reviving and establishing the name and fame of Olavus Petri, for by his archival researches, studies, and writings he had brought the Reformer to light anew and prompted a deeper appreciation of his life work.

The most characteristic traits of the spirit and style of Olavus Petri, as found in his literary works, are, his terse and forceful language, his calm, clear objectivity, his severe earnestness, his implicit faith and trust in the Scriptures, and his deep longing for eternal rest and peace. While these characteristics were the peculiar gifts of God to him, they were doubtless molded to some extent by the nature of the country and the general traits of the nation to which he belonged.

The Augustana Synod owes a debt of gratitude and veneration to this noble Reformer, not only for his part in the shaping of the language handed down to us as a rich heritage from our forefathers, but our greatest obligations are due for the fundamental work laid down by him on the liturgy and order of service of our Evangelical Lutheran Church, and for his preaching of the saving gospel of Christ. May we all emulate the example of the great Reformer in sanctified earnestness, manly sense of duty, sincere faith, and unswerving adherence to the eternal truth of justification by faith in Christ Jesus. As members of a true Lutheran free Church, we will then prosper in this new free land of ours, in our God-given calling, to keep and to confess the pure and unfalsified Word of God. If we do this, in sincere hearts confessing Christ as our Lord and Saviour, He will keep his sure promise: "Because thou didst keep the word of my patience, I also will keep thee from the hour of trial, that hour which is to come upon the whole world, to try them that dwell upon the earth." Rev. 3: 10.

INDEX

CORRECTIONS

Page 54, line 13. Read: —— visits to the sick, funeral services at the grave, and the preparation — —

Page 70, line 17. Read: —— priests and by "the false Sture," an adventurer pretending to be the eldest son of Sten Sture the younger, the Dalecarlians — — —

CPSIA information can be obtained
at www.ICGtesting.com
Printed in the USA
LVOW13*2315020418
572081LV00004B/42/P